Watch it Grow

A Chicken's Life

Nancy Dickmann

www.raintreepublishers.co.uk
Visit our website to find out
more information about
Raintree books.

To order:

☎ Phone 0845 6044371

▤ Fax +44 (0) 1865 312263

✉ Email myorders@raintreepublishers.co.uk

Customers from outside the UK please telephone +44 1865 312262

Raintree is an imprint of Capstone Global Library Limited,
a company incorporated in England and Wales having its
registered office at 7 Pilgrim Street, London, EC4V 6LB
– Registered company number: 6695582

Text © Capstone Global Library Limited 2010
First published in hardback in 2010
The moral rights of the proprietor have been asserted.

Edited by Nancy Dickmann, Rebecca Rissman, and Catherine Veitch
Designed by Joanna Hinton-Malivoire
Picture research by Mica Brancic
Production by Victoria Fitzgerald
Originated by Capstone Global Library Ltd
Printed and bound in China by South China Printing
Company Ltd

ISBN 978 0 431 19534 6
14 13 12 11 10
10 9 8 7 6 5 4 3 2 1

British Library Cataloguing in Publication Data
Dickmann, Nancy.
Chicken. -- (Watch it grow)
571.8'18625-dc22

Acknowledgements
We would would like to thank the following for permission to reproduce
photographs: Alamy pp. **5** (© Paul Glendell), **7** (© Vladimir Alexeev), **15**
(© Vladimir Alexeev); FLPA p. **20** (© Peter E. Smith); iStockphoto pp. **8**
(© Andreas Karelias), **9** (© Lisa Mory), **10** (© Leszek Dudzik), **13** (© Cindy
Singleton), **14 main** (© David de Groot), **16** (© Danish Khan), **17**
(© Denice Breaux), **18** (© Eli Franssens), **19** (© Tony Campbell), **21**
(© Smitt), **22 top** (© Lisa Mory), **22 left** (© Leszek Dudzik), **22 bottom**
(© Denice Breaux), **23 top** (© Cindy Singleton), **23 middle top**
(© Eli Franssens), **23 bottom** (© Tony Campbell); Photolibrary pp. **4**
(Superstock/© Hill Creek Pictures), **6** (age fotostock/© Alberto Paredes),
11 (Superstock/© SUPERSTOCK INC), **12** (© Oxford Scientific (OSF)), **22
right** (© Oxford Scientific (OSF)), **23 middle bottom** (© Oxford Scientific
(OSF)); Shutterstock p. **14 inset** (© Vinicius Tupinamba).

Front cover photograph (main) of hens in a farmyard reproduced with
permission of Photoalto (© Yves Regaldi). Front cover photograph (inset)
of a brown egg reproduced with permission of iStockphoto (© Lisa Mory).
Back cover photograph of a chicken hatching reproduced with permission
of Photolibrary (© Oxford Scientific).

The publisher would like to thank Nancy Harris for her assistance in the
preparation of this book.

Every effort has been made to contact copyright holders of material
reproduced in this book. Any omissions will be rectified in subsequent
printings if notice is given to the publisher.

Contents

Life cycles

All living things have a life cycle.

Chickens have a life cycle.

egg

A chick hatches from an egg.

It grows up.

A chicken lays eggs.
Later it will die.

Eggs

A female chicken is called a hen.

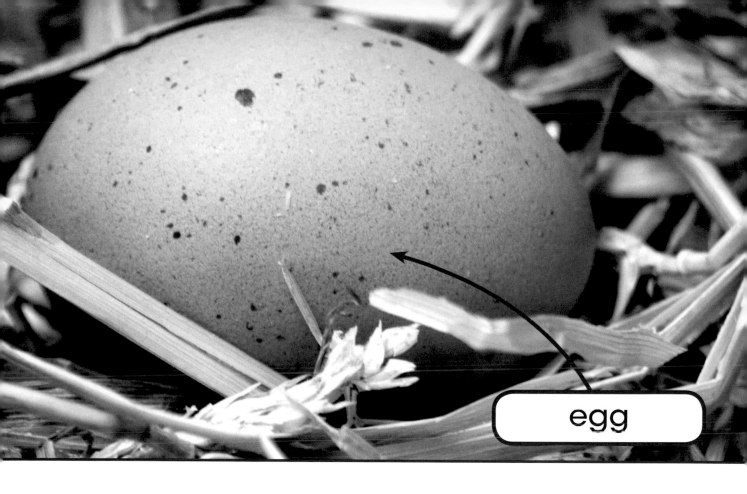

egg

A hen lays eggs.

The hen sits on the eggs to keep
them warm.

A baby chick is inside each egg.

Chicks

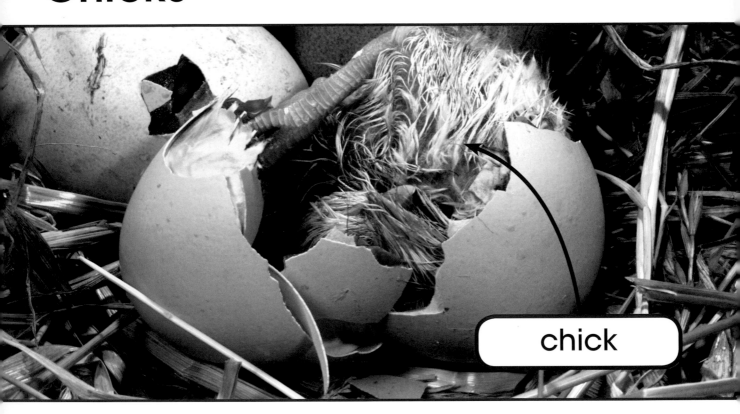

chick

The chick hatches from the egg.

feathers

The chick has yellow feathers.

worm

The chick eats worms and insects.

The mother hen keeps her
chicks safe.

The chick grows bigger.

The chick's feathers turn white.

Becoming a chicken

cockerel

A male chick grows into a cockerel.

A female chick grows into a hen.

The hen lays eggs.

The life cycle starts again.

Life cycle of a chicken

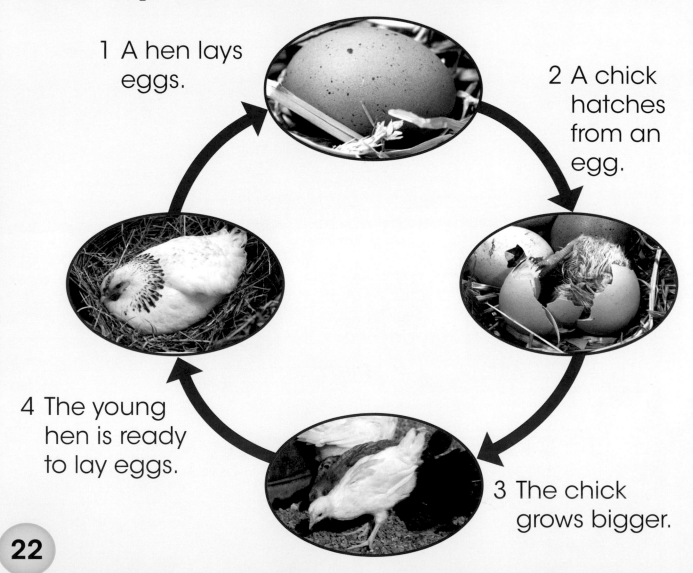

1 A hen lays eggs.

2 A chick hatches from an egg.

3 The chick grows bigger.

4 The young hen is ready to lay eggs.

Picture glossary

 **chick** young chicken. A chick has yellow feathers and hatches from an egg.

 **cockerel** male chicken

 **hatch** to be born from an egg

 **hen** female chicken. Hens can lay eggs.

Index

Notes to parents and teachers

Before reading

Show the children a hen's egg and ask them if they know what laid it. Tell them that all birds lay eggs and look at some pictures of different sized and coloured eggs together.

After reading

• In the spring you could try hatching some chicks. You will need some fertile chicken eggs and an incubator, as well as a home for the hatched chicks to go to. Explain to the children that the incubator keeps the eggs warm like a mother hen. Get the children to help you turn the eggs three times a day (this also needs to happen at the weekend). Ask the children to count the days until each egg hatches and whether they know how the chicks get out of the eggs. Make sure children handle the chicks gently and wash their hands afterwards.

• Read *Handa's Hen* by Eileen Browne together. Talk about what Mondi would have done to look after her chicks while Handa and Akeyo searched for her. Talk about the other animals in the book, such as the butterflies and the frogs, and their life cycles. Make pictures or masks of the animals in the story and act it out together.